The Brontë Connec...

Ann Dinsdale

HENDON PUBLISHING COMPANY
2007

Published by Hendon Publishing Company
Hendon Mill, Nelson, Lancashire BB9 8AD

ISBN 978 0 86067 1596

Designed by Stubbs Design, Ilkley

Printed by Kolorco, Bradford

Front cover: A view of Haworth Main Street taken in 1899.

Title page: A view of Haworth, 1899.

Back cover: The Red House, Gomersal, home of Charlotte
Brontë's school friends, Mary and Martha Taylor.

CONTENTS

INTRODUCTION

The first illustrated edition of the Brontës' novels, published by Smith, Elder & Co., appeared in 1872 – twenty-five years after the publication of *Jane Eyre* and *Wuthering Heights*. The commissioned artist had been supplied with a list of original locations provided by Charlotte's school friend, Ellen Nussey, and it was announced in the advertisement for the new edition that the places described by the Brontës in their works of fiction were actual places. Thus it was established from early on that the settings of all the Brontë novels had real-life counterparts. The Brontë Society was founded in 1893, and a strong topographical interest in the Brontës' lives and works is reflected in the papers and articles which made a regular appearance in the Society's journal. In 1902 the Society published Herbert Wroot's *Sources of Charlotte Brontë's Novels: Persons and Places*, and excursions to places of Brontë interest became a regular feature of the Society's activities.

Charlotte, Emily and Anne did, of course, rely on their own experience and memories of places they had known in the writing of their novels. Charlotte's letters indicate that she would often take real people and places as a starting point for her fiction – to invest her work with what she called 'the germ of the real'. This is not to deny the Brontës' powers of creativity however, for Charlotte also insisted that 'we only suffer reality to suggest, never to dictate'.

Thornfield Hall and Wuthering Heights may be houses of the imagination, but their descriptions are coloured by memories of real houses, and the photographs selected here provide a fascinating visual record of places which are associated with the Brontës' lives and works. In the intervening years some of these places have changed almost beyond recognition, whilst others no longer exist.

Ann Dinsdale, 2007

The Old Parsonage, Market Street, Thornton, c.1900

In 1815 Mr and Mrs Brontë moved into the Parsonage at Thornton with their two eldest daughters, Maria and Elizabeth. It was here that the four famous Brontë children were born in quick succession: Charlotte (1816), Branwell (1817), Emily (1818) and Anne (1820). In the early 1900s the frontage of the house was extended to incorporate a butcher's shop (as shown in this photograph) and towards the end of the century the building became a restaurant before being converted into two separate dwellings. These have now been reunited, and the current owner has undertaken the task of restoration. At the time of writing however, the building is for sale and its future uncertain.

The Old Bell Chapel, Thornton, pre. 1870

The Brontë family lived at Thornton from 1815-1820 and during this time the seventeenth century Bell Chapel was renovated and a cupola was added. Elizabeth, Charlotte, Branwell, Emily and Anne Brontë were all baptized here. In 1870 the church of St James was built across the road. The Old Bell Chapel was abandoned and now lies in picturesque ruins.

Haworth Church and Parsonage, c.1860

The Brontës moved from Thornton to Haworth in 1820, when Mr Brontë was appointed Perpetual Curate of the Church. Haworth Parsonage remained the family's home for over forty years, and it was here that the famous Brontë novels were written. With the exception of the tower, the Church was demolished and rebuilt in 1879-1881, and a large gabled wing was added to the Parsonage during the same period. The Parsonage served as home to four of Mr Brontë's successors before becoming the Brontë Parsonage Museum in 1928.

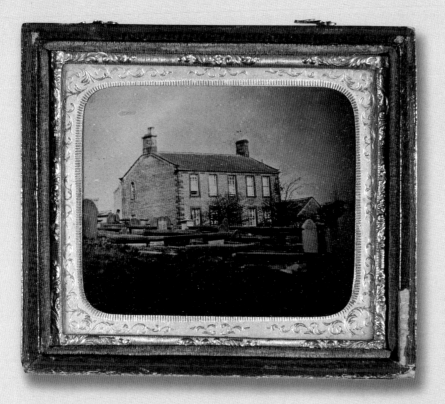

Haworth Parsonage, c.1860

This photograph is likely to have been taken when the Parsonage was still home to Mr Brontë and his widowed son in law, Arthur Bell Nicholls. The open window marks the room where Charlotte died in 1855. The barn, just visible to the right of this photo, served as a stonemason's chipping shed and was demolished in 1903. By the end of the nineteenth century the churchyard had extended into the grassed area shown in the foreground of the photo, and a new cemetery was built on the outskirts of the village.

Top of Main Street, 1899

The crowded summit of Haworth's steep Main Street has changed very little since the mid-nineteenth century. In the Brontës' day, the building next to the church steps was an ironmonger's shop run by William Hartley, who also acted as village postmaster. Facing down the street is the Yorkshire Penny Bank, which at the time this photograph was taken, housed the Brontë Society's first museum on the upper floor.

Haworth Main Street, pre. 1870

This is one of the earliest known images of Haworth's much-photographed Main Street, with its higgledy-piggledy cottages and ginnels, looking much as the Brontës would have known it. The building to the left is a linen draper's shop run by James Ogden, whilst the white-washed cottages, long since demolished, were occupied by James Whitham, a carrier, who at one time courted the Brontë servant Martha Brown, and Simeon Townend, a cabinet-maker.

Haworth Old Hall, 1920

Haworth Old Hall was built in the late sixteenth or early seventeenth century, and is one of the oldest and most striking buildings in Haworth. Situated just below the Main Street, it would have been a familiar sight to the Brontës. This photograph dates from 1920 when the Hall served as Wuthering Heights in the first film adaptation of Emily's novel, made by the Ideal Film Company and starring Milton Rosmer and Anne Trevor. Nowadays the Old Hall is a public house.

Middle Withens, c.1900

There were originally three farms named Withens:
Lower, Middle and Top Withens. Fearing sewage
seepage to their recently constructed reservoirs,
the local water authority bought up the moorland
farms in the late nineteenth century and allowed
them to decay as they fell empty. Middle Withens,
a farmhouse which would have been familiar to
the Brontës, has disappeared completely. It is
believed that the group shown here are the
Haworth Ramblers.

Top Withens, c.1900

This isolated farmhouse about four miles from Haworth Parsonage has entered Brontë mythology as the inspiration for Wuthering Heights in Emily's novel. Throughout the nineteenth century the house was occupied by members of the Sunderland family, some of whom are buried in the churchyard at Haworth. Although it's possible that Emily had the moorland setting of Withens in mind when she wrote her novel, even when complete, the house bore very little resemblance to her description of The Heights.

Ponden Hall, Stanbury, c.1890

Ponden Hall lies in a valley, about two miles from Haworth, and is popularly associated with Thrushcross Grange in *Wuthering Heights*. The seventeenth-century hall was home to generations of the Heaton family, traditional trustees of Haworth Church and possessors of a fine library. It has been suggested that the Brontës borrowed books from Ponden, and they would certainly have been familiar with tales of past Heaton tragedies. Although one of the more impressive houses of the area, Ponden is more homely than the Linton home described in Emily's novel. Ponden Hall is a private house, undergoing restoration by its current owners.

The Old House at Ponden, c.1940s

The 'Old House', sometimes known as Scotchman's Farm, was a former Heaton family residence standing opposite Ponden Hall across a bridle-track. The house would still have been intact in Emily Brontë's day and has been suggested as another possible model for Wuthering Heights. Part of the building has been rebuilt as Ponden House and offers guest accommodation.

Ponden Kirk, c.1910

Penistone Crag, a rocky outcrop situated a mile and a half above Wuthering Heights in Emily's novel, was a childhood haunt of Catherine Earnshaw and Heathcliff. There is a Penistone Hill on the moors behind Haworth Parsonage, but the Crag has been identified as Ponden Kirk, situated on the moors above Stanbury. A small cave-like passage, reminiscent of the Fairy Cave at Penistone Crag, runs through Ponden Kirk, and a local legend claims that anyone who passes through will be married within a year.

Cowan Bridge, c.1900

With six children to educate on a limited income, the recently opened school for the daughters of impoverished clergymen at Cowan Bridge, near Kirkby Lonsdale, must have seemed an ideal solution to Mr Brontë. In 1824 Maria and Elizabeth were dispatched to the school, followed shortly after by Charlotte and Emily. The school regime was harsh, and first Maria, then Elizabeth, was sent home in ill health, where they died within a few weeks of each other. Charlotte later immortalized Cowan Bridge as Lowood in *Jane Eyre*. The school was moved to a healthier situation at Casterton, where it flourishes today. Part of the old school buildings form a row of cottages (shown here), although the dormitory wing was destroyed by fire long ago.

Roe Head, Mirfield, c.1860

In 1831 Charlotte went as a pupil to Miss Wooler's school at Roe Head, Mirfield, where she met her lifelong friends Ellen Nussey and Mary Taylor. She spent eighteen months here, returning as a teacher in 1835. Emily and Anne also attended Roe Head for varying periods, and this photograph shows the building as it would have looked during their time. Roe Head has since been extended and currently houses a special needs school, Holly Bank.

St. Peter's, Hartshead, pre. 1881

The small Norman church of St. Peter's at Hartshead is less than a mile away
from Roe Head. In 1811 Patrick Brontë was appointed minister here, a post
he held for four years, during which time he married Maria Branwell and
their two eldest daughters were born. Mr Brontë's tales of Luddite violence in
the area formed the backdrop to Charlotte's novel *Shirley*, and the Evangelical
Hammond Roberson, a former incumbent at Hartshead and friend of her
father's, provided a model for Matthewson Helstone in the novel. This
photograph shows the church before extensive renovations were carried out
in 1881.

Rydings, Birstall, c.1890

In September 1832 Charlotte visited Ellen Nussey for the first time at her family home, Rydings at Birstall. Branwell, acting as her escort, was so impressed by the castellated house set among ancient trees that he told Charlotte he was leaving her in paradise. Ellen believed that Rydings had provided the inspiration for Thornfield in *Jane Eyre*. Although the house has been preserved externally, the internal features have been swept away and the building converted to a conference centre, owned by the paint company whose industrial units surround the house.

Brookroyd, Birstall, c.1900

In 1836, following the death of Ellen's father, reduced circumstances forced the Nusseys to leave Rydings and move into the less impressive Brookroyd. Charlotte visited Brookroyd many times and is said to have corrected the proofs of *Jane Eyre* here on one occasion. Although hemmed in by a modern housing development, Brookroyd still remains as a private residence.

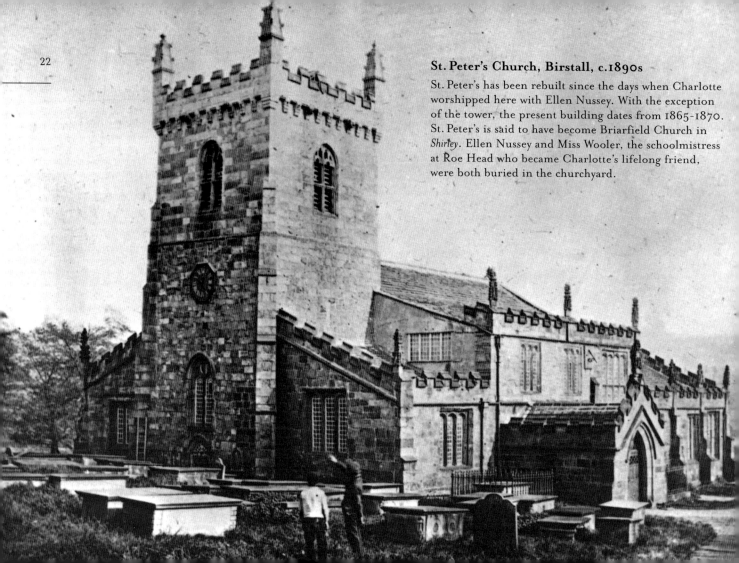

St. Peter's Church, Birstall, c.1890s

St. Peter's has been rebuilt since the days when Charlotte worshipped here with Ellen Nussey. With the exception of the tower, the present building dates from 1865-1870. St. Peter's is said to have become Briarfield Church in *Shirley*. Ellen Nussey and Miss Wooler, the schoolmistress at Roe Head who became Charlotte's lifelong friend, were both buried in the churchyard.

Red House, Gomersal, c.1910

The Red House at Gomersal was the home of the Taylor family, woollen cloth merchants and manufacturers. Charlotte stayed here with her school friends, Mary and Martha Taylor, and the house served as the model for Briarmains, home of the Yorke family in her novel *Shirley*. The house is now a museum and the stained glass windows, described in *Shirley*, are still to be seen in the dining room.

Oakwell Hall, Birstall, c.1930

Oakwell Hall is an Elizabethan manor house which Charlotte would have known from her visits to Birstall. Oakwell, which featured as Fieldhead, the home of the heroine in her novel *Shirley*, has a fascinating history irrespective of its Brontë connection, and like the Red House, it is open to the public.

Law Hill, Southowram, c.1900

In 1838, Law Hill at Southowram, near Halifax, was a girls' school run by Miss Patchett.
Emily taught here for six months and in a letter, Charlotte described her sister's
duties as 'hard labour from six in the morning until near eleven at night, with only
one half-hour of exercise between.'

Law Hill (rear view), c.1900

Whilst at Law Hill, Emily is likely to have heard the story of its builder, Jack Sharp, a Heathcliff-like figure who attempted to usurp the property and fortunes of his adopted family – a story which may well have played a part in the creation of *Wuthering Heights*. Today Law Hill is a private house.

High Sunderland Hall, Southowram, c.1910

High Sunderland Hall was a gaunt seventeenth century mansion standing on an exposed hillside outside Halifax. Emily would have known the house from her time as teacher at nearby Law Hill. One of the striking features of High Sunderland Hall was the carving embellishing the façade. It's likely that Emily drew on such architectural details in creating Wuthering Heights.

Gateway at High Sunderland, c.1910

At the time Emily would have known High Sunderland it was occupied by tenant farmers and falling into a state of decay. Mining in the area is said to have weakened the building's foundations, and although attempts were made to save the house, it seems likely that its ruinous state made demolition inevitable. All that survives of High Sunderland today is some of the decorative stonework, preserved at Shibden Hall Museum in Halifax.

Blake Hall, Mirfield, c.1900

From April to December, 1839, Anne went as governess to the two eldest children of Joshua and Mary Ingham at Blake Hall, Mirfield, near Leeds. According to Charlotte, Anne found her charges to be 'desperate little dunces' and was not allowed by the parents to discipline the children herself. The obnoxious Bloomfields in her first novel, *Agnes Grey*, are said to be based on the Ingham family. Blake Hall was demolished in 1954 and the site is now occupied by the Blake Hall housing estate.

Stonegappe, Lothersdale, c.1900

In May 1839 Charlotte went as governess to the Sidgwick family at Stonegappe, Lothersdale, near Skipton. Her time there was brief and unhappy, and in a letter written to Emily, Charlotte wrote: 'I have striven hard to be pleased with my new situation. The country, the house, and the grounds are, as I have said, divine. But, alack-a-day! there is such a thing as seeing all beautiful around you – pleasant woods, winding white paths, green lawns, and blue sunshiny sky – and not having a free moment or a free thought left to enjoy them in.' It is often claimed that when Charlotte came to write *Jane Eyre*, Stonegappe served as the model for Gateshead, home of the Reed family. The house remains a private residence.

Stonegappe, Lothersdale.
The "Gateshead Hall"
of "Jane Eyre".

Norton Conyers, Ripon, c.1890

During her time as governess to the Sidgwick family, Charlotte is likely to
have visited Norton Conyers near Ripon, home of the Graham family, which
was rented for a time by Mrs Sidgwick's brother, Frederick Greenwood.
Norton Conyers is one of several suggested originals for Thornfield Hall in
Jane Eyre, for although there are no references to visiting the house in Charlotte's
surviving correspondence, her friend Ellen Nussey remembered 'receiving
from Charlotte Brontë a verbal description of the place and recalled the
impression made on Charlotte by the story of the mad woman confined to
the attic'.

Easton House, Bridlington, pre. 1961

In 1839 Charlotte and Ellen Nussey spent four happy weeks staying with Mr and Mrs Hudson at Easton House, near Bridlington (formerly Burlington). The Hudsons were acquaintances of Ellen's family, and during her stay, Charlotte produced watercolour paintings depicting both her hostess and Easton House. She returned under less happy circumstances following the death of Anne Brontë in 1849. Easton House was demolished in 1961 and East Field Farm now stands on the site.

Upperwood House, Rawdon, c.1890

For most of 1841 Charlotte was governess to the White family of Upperwood House, Rawdon, near Bradford. In a letter to her friend Ellen Nussey, Charlotte wrote: 'The house is not very large, but exceedingly comfortable, and well regulated; the grounds are fine and extensive. In taking this place I have made a large sacrifice in the way of salary, in the hope of securing ... the society of cheerful faces, and minds and hearts not dug out of a lead-mine, or cut from a marble quarry.'

Rear view of Upperwood House, c.1890

Upperwood House was demolished in the late nineteenth century and nowadays Brontë House, the preparatory school for Woodhouse Grove, stands in its place. A surviving portico has been incorporated into a summer-house in the grounds.

Hathersage Vicarage, c.1960

In the summer of 1845, Charlotte and Ellen Nussey stayed at the vicarage in Hathersage, Derbyshire, which was being renovated before the return of the vicar, Ellen's brother Henry, and his bride. Henry had been casting around for a suitable wife for some years and had once proposed marriage to Charlotte. The extension he built to include a bay windowed sitting room and two bedrooms above can be seen to the left on this photograph.

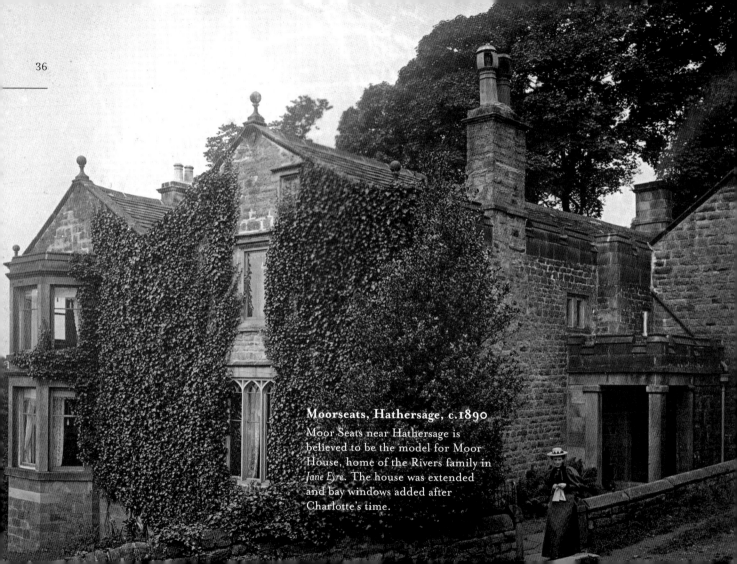

Moorseats, Hathersage, c.1890
Moor Seats near Hathersage is
believed to be the model for Moor
House, home of the Rivers family in
Jane Eyre. The house was extended
and bay windows added after
Charlotte's time.

North Lees Hall, Hathersage, c.1960

During their stay at Hathersage, Charlotte and Ellen Nussey visited North Lees Hall, an Elizabethan manor house which was home to the Eyre family. It is often claimed that North Lees provided the inspiration for Thornfield Hall in *Jane Eyre*, and it was also here that Charlotte saw the Apostles' cupboard, described in chapter 20 of the novel. Nowadays North Lees Hall is divided into two holiday apartments owned by The Vivat Trust.

59 Boundary Street West (formerly 83 Mount Pleasant), Manchester, c.1900

In August 1846 Charlotte accompanied her father to Manchester, where he was to undergo an operation for the removal of a cataract. They took lodgings in this house, and whilst her father convalesced in a darkened room, Charlotte began writing *Jane Eyre*. The site was badly damaged during the air raids which took place in December 1940, and had been levelled by 1945.

Wycoller Hall, c.1890

Wycoller Hall, a sixteenth century manor house near Colne, has become established
in the popular imagination as Ferndean Manor, the house to which Rochester
retreated after Thornfield was destroyed by fire in *Jane Eyre*. Although it seems likely,
we do not know for certain that the Brontës ever visited Wycoller. In *The Life of Charlotte
Brontë* Mrs Gaskell recounts tales concerning the eccentric squire of Wycoller which

Fireplace at Wycoller Hall, c.1890

This wonderful arched fireplace is still to be seen amidst the picturesque ruins of Wycoller Hall. It was built after Henry Owen Cunliffe inherited the Hall in 1773 and added many impressive mock-Jacobean features to the building. After his death in 1818 the Hall remained uninhabited and was allowed to fall into disrepair.

No.2, The Cliff, Scarborough, pre.1863

Branwell and Emily died of tuberculosis in 1848 and it soon became clear that Anne was also ill. In an attempt to prolong her life, Anne went to Scarborough on the Yorkshire coast, accompanied by Charlotte and Ellen Nussey. They lodged at No.2, The Cliff (believed to be one of the cottages next to the large building on the right of this photograph), where Anne had stayed on previous visits with the Robinson family, and where she died on 28 May 1849. The house was demolished and the site is now occupied by the Grand Hotel.

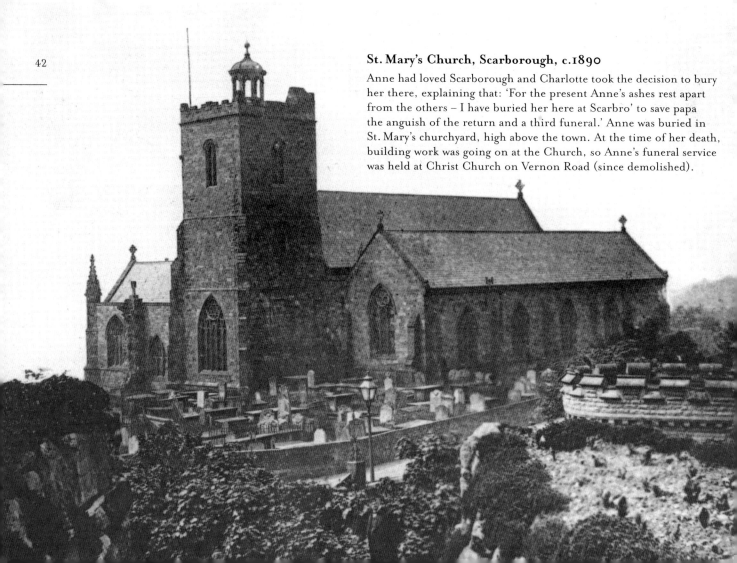

St. Mary's Church, Scarborough, c.1890

Anne had loved Scarborough and Charlotte took the decision to bury her there, explaining that: 'For the present Anne's ashes rest apart from the others – I have buried her here at Scarbro' to save papa the anguish of the return and a third funeral.' Anne was buried in St. Mary's churchyard, high above the town. At the time of her death, building work was going on at the Church, so Anne's funeral service was held at Christ Church on Vernon Road (since demolished).

Anne Brontë's grave, Scarborough, c.1890

Three years after Anne's death, Charlotte re-visited her sister's grave at Scarborough. In a letter she wrote: 'On Friday I went to Scarboro', visited the church-yard and stone – it must be refaced and re-lettered – there are 5 errors.' One of the errors still remains, for Anne's age at death is given as twenty-eight instead of twenty-nine.

Cliff House, Filey, c.1890s

After Anne's death, Charlotte and Ellen found the crowds at Scarborough 'too gay' and moved to Filey where they lodged at Cliff House. Cliff House is currently a combined café and shop, bearing a wall plaque to alert visitors to its Brontë connection.

Briery Close, near Windermere, c.1890s

In August 1850 Charlotte stayed at Briery Close near Windermere, the summer residence of Sir James and Lady Kay-Shuttleworth of Gawthorpe Hall at Padiham. It was here that she met the novelist Elizabeth Gaskell, which resulted in a friendship that lasted the remaining five years of Charlotte's life and produced one of the most popular biographies ever written, *The Life of Charlotte Brontë*, published in 1857. Little has survived of the original house.

The Knoll, Ambleside, c.1890s

The Knoll at Ambleside in the Lake District was built in 1845 by the formidable social reformer and writer Harriet Martineau. Charlotte stayed here in December 1850 after having met Harriet in London the previous year. In 1853 Martineau's review of *Villette* hurt Charlotte deeply and caused her to break off the friendship. The Knoll has since been divided into two dwellings, although its external appearance remains virtually unchanged.

84 Plymouth Grove, Manchester, c.1900

Charlotte visited the Gaskells' comfortable home in Manchester on three occasions. Nowadays it's difficult to envisage the house that Charlotte described as '... a large, cheerful, airy house, quite out of Manchester smoke; a garden surrounds it, and, as in this hot weather the windows were kept open, a whispering of leaves and perfume of flowers always pervaded the rooms.' After years of neglect, the building is now owned by Manchester Historic Buildings Trust and currently awaiting restoration.

Haworth Old Church interior with Brontë plaque, pre.1879

Apart from Anne, who was buried at Scarborough, the Brontës were all laid to rest in a family vault beneath the floor of the chancel of Haworth church. The family's memorial plaque is clearly visible in this early photo showing the interior of the church with its three-decker pulpit and oak box pews. When the Church was demolished in 1879, the Brontë vault was concreted over but otherwise left undisturbed. The new church, consecrated in 1881, was rebuilt on the same site.